IMAGES
of America

PATRICK AIR
FORCE BASE

Patrick Air Force Base (AFB) is bordered on the east by the Atlantic Ocean and on the west by the Banana River. The base is 4.1 miles long and 1.25 miles across at its widest point. It comprises approximately 1,790 acres and is located in an area known as Florida's Space Coast just south of the city of Cocoa Beach, Florida.

ON THE COVER: Against a backdrop of missiles and the impressive Air Force Technical Laboratory at Patrick AFB, swimmers enjoy a pool located adjacent to the Non-Commissioned Officers (NCO) Club. The facility offered entertainment, food, and recreation. Funded by club members, the pool provided a fun way for the NCOs and their families to escape the heat of a Florida summer.

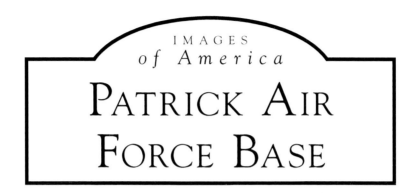

IMAGES
of America

PATRICK AIR FORCE BASE

Roger McCormick
Foreword by Maj. Gen. Everett H. Thomas, USAF, Ret.

ARCADIA
PUBLISHING

Published by Arcadia Publishing
Charleston, South Carolina

Printed in the United States of America

Library of Congress Control Number: 2016933940

For all general information, please contact Arcadia Publishing:
Telephone 843-853-2070
Fax 843-853-0044
E-mail sales@arcadiapublishing.com
For customer service and orders:
Toll-Free 1-888-313-2665

Visit us on the Internet at www.arcadiapublishing.com

*Dedicated to the men and women, military and
civilian, past and present, of Patrick AFB.
Keep 'em flying . . . go for launch . . . go Sharks!*

CONTENTS

FOREWORD

I began my military career in the US Air Force with a commission through the Reserve Officers' Training Corps program in 1980. During my 33 years with the Air Force, I have served as commander at the squadron, group, and wing levels. From snowstorms at Whiteman AFB in Missouri to brutally hot days at Nellis AFB in Nevada, I've been stationed across the United States. I completed several tours at the Pentagon and have traveled from coast to coast, including the territory of Guam.

Among my most memorable tours was my first assignment at Patrick AFB in 1995 as commander of Cape Canaveral AFS. After a year, I began serving as commander of the 5th Space Launch Squadron, which involved hands-on technical procedures with Titan rockets. There is nothing quite as exciting or exhilarating as being involved in the process of preparing a rocket for launch and then watching the rocket lift off. Whether the rocket is carrying a military payload to help troops in distant regions of the world or a probe to explore our solar system, it's always awe-inspiring.

I was fortunate to return to Patrick AFB in 2003 as vice commander of the 45th Space Wing. During my two-year tour, I bought a house near Patrick, somehow knowing that someday I would return for good. Since retiring in 2013, I have been associated with several aerospace companies in various parts of the country. However, I can't seem to get the sand out of my shoes; Florida keeps calling me back. I am looking forward to a few rounds at the Manatee Cove Golf Course and a cool beverage at the Tiki Bar at the marina.

Thanks to the tireless efforts of Roger McCormick, we now have a photographic chronicle of Patrick AFB as it grew up. With more than 27 years at the Air Force Space & Missile Museum and 23 years working the Space Shuttle program, Roger has been a persistent advocate for all things space: past, present, and future. Get ready to enter the "World's Premier Gateway to Space"—I'm sure you'll enjoy the ride.

—Maj. Gen. Everett H. Thomas, USAF, Ret.

ACKNOWLEDGMENTS

I am thankful for all the people who helped make this book possible. The following individuals in particular deserve special recognition: Emily Perry, director, Air Force Space & Missile Museum, for her proofreading, editing, and content management expertise; Col. John Hilliard, USAF, Ret., for his wealth of knowledge concerning the subject matter and for countless trips escorting me onto Patrick AFB to conduct research; Ray Heard, historian, 45th Space Wing, Patrick AFB, for assistance with research and utilizing the photographic archive at the base; Ben DiBiase, director, educational resources, Florida Historical Society, for assistance with research and locating rare photographs pertaining to Banana River Naval Air Station; and Maj. Gen. Everett H. Thomas, USAF, Ret., for writing the foreword.

Liz Gurley, senior title manager, and the staff of Arcadia Publishing, merit recognition for their support and great patience. Other individuals, organizations, and repositories contributed photographs, recollections, encouragement, advice, and invaluable assistance. They are: Andrei Adaryukov, Christopher Calkins, and Connie Morrison, Defense Equal Opportunity Management Institute, Patrick AFB; Deborah Allison, foundation services manager, and Sharon Rodriguez, executive assistant, US Air Force Space & Missile Museum Foundation; Heidi M. Hunt, specialist, and Shawn Walleck, chief, public affairs, Patrick AFB; Dr. Libby Allison, professor, West Texas State University; J.P. "Andy" Anderson, retired communications engineer; Senior Master Sgt. Jim Hale, USAF, Ret.; George "Speedy" Harrell, volunteer, Florida Historical Society; Al Hartmann, space and missile historian; Glenna Holmes, Manatee Cove Marina; Matthey Jurgens, project manager, multimedia, Patrick AFB; Martha Loss, Central Brevard Library & Reference Center; TMC (SS) William J. Scenna, US Navy, Ret.; Major Cathleen Snow, chief, public affairs, 920th Rescue Wing, Patrick AFB; Air Force Space & Missile Museum Archive; Cape Canaveral Public Library; Cocoa Public Library; and Cocoa Beach Public Library.

Unless otherwise noted, all photographs in this book appear courtesy of the 45th Space Wing History Office, Patrick AFB.

The author's royalties from this volume will go to the US Air Force Space & Missile Museum Foundation, PO Box 893, Cape Canaveral, Florida 32920. The foundation is a 501(c)(3) not-for-profit organization, and receives no local, county, or state funds. For more information, please visit www.afspacemuseum.org.

INTRODUCTION

Patrick Air Force Base is currently the administrative headquarters of the 45th Space Wing and its predecessor organizations. Part of Air Force Space Command, the wing is responsible for supervision and support of operations at the base and at launch facilities 15 miles north at Cape Canaveral Air Force Station (CCAFS).

Patrick AFB is located on a narrow strip of land along Highway A1A between the Atlantic Ocean and Banana River in Brevard County, Florida. The base is just south of the city of Cocoa Beach and is part of Florida's Space Coast.

During World War II, the base was a Navy training and seaplane patrol facility called Banana River Naval Air Station (BRNAS). It was transferred to the Air Force in 1948 for establishment of a long-range proving ground in order to test guided missiles. In 1950, it was renamed Patrick AFB in honor of Maj. Gen. Mason M. Patrick, chief of the Army Air Corps from 1921 to 1927.

The decision to start launching missiles from the east coast of Florida was made due to the existing military base nearby to serve as a command and control headquarters, and due to the string of islands downrange in the Atlantic Ocean along the path of most missile launches to serve as tracking stations. Patrick AFB has played a role in thousands of missile tests and rocket launches since 1950. From the early 1970s, it has had a vital role in monitoring nuclear testing around the world. Patrick AFB has promoted the dignity of all races of individuals in the military. It provides services to a large population of retirees in the area. Patrick AFB continues to be involved with military, scientific, and commercial launches, as well as missile tests by the Navy from submarines off the coast.

This book is a tribute to the men and women of Patrick AFB, military and civilian personnel, whose work continues to add to a rich history. This Air Force base, which was once a Navy base, before being named for an Army general, has a unique history and important story to tell about America's national defense and its efforts in space.

One

BANANA RIVER NAVAL AIR STATION

Authorized by the Naval Expansion Act of 1938, BRNAS was commissioned on October 1, 1940, to serve as an adjunct base of Jacksonville Naval Air Station, Florida. Soon after the United States became involved in World War II in 1941, the Navy began conducting anti-submarine patrols along Florida's coast using PBM Mariner and PBY Catalina seaplanes based in part at BRNAS. Later, the PBMs were used only for training purposes when they were replaced on patrol by OS2U Kingfisher aircraft. Other activities at the air station included air search and rescue operations, pilot and bombardier training, operation of a blimp squadron, communications research, an aviation navigation school, and a major aircraft repair and maintenance facility. Project Baker, an experimental training unit at the air station, was a confidential program to develop equipment and test procedures for instrument landings.

On July 9, 1945, a PBM Mariner seaplane on Training Flight No. 36, with a crew of 12, failed to return to BRNAS from a six-hour patrol mission to Great Exuma Island, Bahamas. Five months later on December 5, 1945, Flight No. 19, consisting of five TBM Avenger torpedo bombers and 14 crewmen, went missing after taking off from Fort Lauderdale Naval Air Station, Florida. A PBM from BRNAS, with 13 crewmen, took off in search of the torpedo bombers. The PBM never returned and is believed to have exploded in midair, but no wreckage was found. None of the planes or crew of Training Flight No. 36 or Flight No. 19 have ever been located; both incidents often appear in stories about mysterious disappearances within the Bermuda Triangle.

BRNAS was deactivated and declared surplus by the Navy on August 1, 1947. On September 1, 1948, the base was transferred to the Air Force in anticipation of activating it as a facility to support missile testing. During the next two years, the former Navy facility underwent several name changes until August 1, 1950, when it received its current name: Patrick AFB.

Construction of BRNAS began in late 1939 with land clearing and well drilling. The work was slow due to the nearly impenetrable palmetto growth and other vegetation covering the ground. An overabundance of mosquitoes in the area created a constant distraction for the work crews.

U.S. NAVAL AIR STATION
BANANA RIVER, FLA.

With numerous buildings still under construction, and no aircraft yet assigned to the base, BRNAS was commissioned on October 1, 1940. The logo for the base, shown on this vintage matchbook cover, portrays a duck with a pilot's headset and goggles landing on the water similar to a seaplane. The banana represents the Banana River, for which the base was named. (Author's collection.)

The commissioning ceremony for BRNAS was officiated by Lt. Comdr. Waldo Tullsen. The Naval Academy graduate read orders authorizing the establishment of the air station as part of the Navy. The orders further confirmed Tullsen as the commanding officer. At the time of commissioning, the facility consisted of a single hangar and five other buildings, with no paved sidewalks or roads. (Courtesy of Florida Historical Society.)

No living quarters, eating facilities, or running water were available for personnel assigned to the air station. Sailors were housed in private homes in communities close to the station. One account indicates the drinking water was so bad that the men gladly opted for beer and soft drinks instead. Construction work at the new air station meant jobs for many local residents at a time of high unemployment.

BRNAS was created as an auxiliary landing area for training units based at the air station in Jacksonville, Florida. Due to the high number of training squadrons flying out of the Norfolk, Virginia Naval Air Station, the Navy decided to move some of its squadrons to BRNAS. Landing strips were constructed in 1943, allowing concurrent operations of shore-based aircraft.

Constructed in 1941, Building No. 312 was a seaplane hangar and supported Project Baker at BRNAS. Training squadrons began arriving in 1941 with Patrol Bomber aircraft manufactured by the Martin Company (PBMs). In May 1951, the first security restricted area at Patrick AFB was established. The area encompassed Building No. 312, as well as adjacent grounds, for the assembly and inspection of Matador missiles.

When the United States entered World War II, the role of BRNAS grew in scope and importance. No longer just a base for training flights, it was now involved in the war effort. Patrol missions looking for enemy submarines and performing search and rescue missions for ships that had been attacked were among the new duties. Here, sailors wash down a PBM aircraft. (Courtesy of Florida Historical Society.)

U. S. Naval Air Station, Banana River, Fla.

"Banana River Bounce"

OFFICIAL U. S. NAVY PHOTOGRAPH

This vintage postcard shows a PMB Mariner aircraft coming in for a bumpy landing on the Banana River. Owing its name to the river, BRNAS was sandwiched between the river to the west and the Atlantic Ocean to the east. Approaching aircraft landed in the river and then taxied up concrete ramps at the air station to dry land. (Author's collection.)

A PBM towers over personnel standing nearby inside its hangar at BRNAS. The first PBMs arrived at the air station in August 1941. Prior to the PBMs, the first aircraft on station was a Grumman J2F Duck earlier in 1941. At the time, only BRNAS commander Tullsen was qualified to pilot the Duck, a single-engine amphibious biplane.

The Vought Sikorsky OS2U Kingfisher performed a variety of roles, from search and rescue to patrolling for and attacking submarines. At BRNAS, Kingfishers replaced the larger PBM Mariner seaplanes on patrol in early 1942. The Kingfisher was 34.8 feet long, with a wingspan of 35.8 feet, and carried a crew of two.

Skippy was the beloved mascot of Headquarters Squadron 12 stationed at BRNAS. When Skippy died in September 1943, the squadron planned a proper funeral. Skippy was placed in an empty bomb casing, or "embombed," and attached to the wing of an OS2U Kingfisher, then flown out to sea and dropped. What type of animal Skippy was is unknown, but he or she was important enough to be laid to rest with honor.

PB stands for Patrol Bomber; the third letter designated the company that manufactured the aircraft. In the case of the PBY, the "Y" stands for the Consolidated Aircraft Company. Shown here is the PBY Catalina assigned to BRNAS. The Catalina was a high-wing, twin-engine aircraft classified as a flying boat, as it could land on water or a runway.

JoJo, the 11-month-old mascot of the assembly and repair shop at BRNAS, was reportedly very fond of rides around the base on the scooter shown here. Every time he heard the motor running, he ran toward it wanting a ride. Pictured with Ernest Lindley, a veteran of the Pacific War and repair shop chief, JoJo is standing tall and ready to go with his paws on the handlebars. On many military bases, mascots are often stray animals that wander onto the base and are adopted by those who find them, or perhaps it is the animals that do the adopting. These mascots were usually not approved and were kept in secret by those taking care of them. (Courtesy of Florida Historical Society.)

The first female personnel assigned to BRNAS arrived in January 1944, with a larger contingent arriving by bus the following month. They were members of the Women Accepted for Volunteer Emergency Service (WAVES). The WAVES served in numerous support positions held by sailors, which made the men available for combat duty instead.

BRNAS remained active for two years following World War II. The air station was deactivated in September 1947, and personnel stationed at BRNAS were reassigned to other Navy bases. The seaplane base changed dramatically through the years to become the facility it is today, with the responsibility of missile testing and launching rockets into space. The only thing that has not changed much is the number of mosquitoes in the area.

"This news is old enough,
yet it is every day's news."
—*Shakespeare.*

BANANA PEELINGS

U. S. NAVAL AIR STATION　　·　　·　　·　　BANANA RIVER, FLORIDA

| VOL. 4, NO. 23 | MARCH 8, 1946 | TWELVE PAGES |

New Executive Officer Assumes Duties

CAC Training For Fleet To Continue

"We will continue to train enlisted personnel as long as the Fleet requires them," according to Commander Robert Cox, Officer-in-Charge of the Advanced Training Unit.

Clarifying the enlisted status, Commander Cox advised that, pending cancellation of fleet requirements, enlisted personnel will be trained in conformity with the old training syllabus. The new syllabus, now effective both in ATU and Ground Training, does NOT provide for the schooling of enlisted personnel.

There are off-the-record indications, Comdr. Cox added, that enlisted training aboard this station finally will be discontinued around 1 July. "This" he stressed, "is a strictly unofficial estimate."

The Advanced Training Unit at present is under complement needs. Reductions in personnel, other than those compelled by demobilization, are not now contemplated.

A & R Closes Doors After 5-Year Operation

The Assembly and Repair Unit closed its doors today after five years of operation.

Originally tabled for roll-up on 1 March, final repairs on two F7F's and a PBY engine prevented meeting of the deadline.

A&R's last PBY was transferred to the Air Bomber's Training Unit on Tuesday, 5 March.

"Lips that touch wine shall never touch mine," declared a co-ed. And after she was graduated, she taught school for years and years and years and years.

The teacher wrote on the blackboard: "I don't have no fun at beach" and asked the class, "How should I correct this?"

"Get a boy friend," piped up little Willie.

Mr. Arthur F. James
Local Red Cross Field Director

Base Responds To Red Cross Appeal

Banana River's 1946 Red Cross Campaign made an excellent start on 1 March, with chiefly non-solicited contributions beginning to fill the 20-odd containers scattered strategically throughout the station.

Solicitation of officers and civilian employees was being conducted departmentally, with an officer in each division appointed to supervise the collection.

The Fund Campaign manager, Lieutenant Commander C. D. Heldt, USNR, Welfare Officer and local Red Cross Director Arthur F. James, pointed out that no definite quota has been established for the drive. It was expected, however, that the campaign would equal or exceed the funds grossed for the March of Dimes.

Said one smooth sailor to one cute trick at a USO dance: "Tell me about yourself—your struggles, your dreams, your telephone number."

Commander Hastings, USN, Was Former Melbourne C.O.

Commander Willard E. Hastings, USN, assumed the duties of Executive Officer on 6 March, 1946.

Commander Hastings, Commanding Officer of NAS Melbourne, Florida, until its official shut-down on 22 February, began his distinguished naval career after graduation from the Naval Academy in 1934.

He was transferred to the USS Nevada, serving in virtually all capacities until his reassignment to Pensacola in the Spring of 1937 for flight training. He received his wings in May, 1938, and was shifted to Squadron VB#2 aboard the much-storied flattop USS Lexington.

In September, 1940, Commander Hastings returned to Pensacola as Officer-in-Charge of the Navy Photographic School. In October, 1942, he was shunted to Newport News, Virginia, for the commissioning of the new CV USS Essex. He functioned as Operations Officer and later as Assistant Air Officer of the Essex until January, 1944, when he was transferred to Astoria, Oregon, for the commissioning of the Rudyerd Bay. He served as Air Officer of the Bay until July, 1945, when he was attached to the Radar School, St. Simons Island, Georgia.

Commander Hastings served as Commanding Officer of NAS Green Cove Springs from September to December, 1945, when he was reassigned to NAS Melbourne.

Navy Relief Office Transferred Here

On 14 February, the headquarters of the local branch of the Navy Relief Society was transferred from NAS Sanford to this station and became known as the Banana River Auxiliary Navy Relief Society.

Under the direction of Captain William J. Slattery, Commanding Officer and President of the Auxiliary Branch, and Lieutenant (jg) Herbert Bailey, Secretary-Treasurer, an office has been set-up in room 106 of the Administration Building. Sylveria M. Graff, Y3/c, has been designated Navy Relief Yeoman. H. P. Tapia, S1/c, formerly the Chaplain's Yeoman at Sanford, has been temporarily attached to this station to assist in opening the office.

New Flight Syllabus Excludes Small Links

Small Link Trainers, long an integral part of Ground Training, shut down on 1 March when the new ground school training syllabus became effective.

The new syllabus contains no provision for Small Link instruction.

However, according to Lieutenant Corinne Van Iderstine (WR), Link Officer, "two Link Trainers will be available for such station personnel as desire instrument time." Three Link Operators (SpT) have been retained for this function.

"You certainly gave me a bum steer," said the milkmaid as she came back with an empty pail.

PSC Transfer Figures Bared for Feb., March

With no changes in demobilization other than the previously announced cut to 28 points for enlisted male personnel on 2 May, the Station Personnel Officer has released the following figures, valid as of 2 March:

Some 399 men have been transferred to Personnel Separation Centers in the last 23 days. This includes 158 on 15 February and 241 on 2 March.

Banana Peelings, the newspaper for BRNAS, was published twice a month by the officers and others assigned to the station. The newspaper was printed at no cost to the Navy and distributed free to all station personnel. *Banana Peelings* was a member of the Ship's Editorial Association and the Camp Newspaper Service. Each issue featured stories from various bases in the Navy, local announcements, coverage and scores of intra-station sporting events, a book review section, cartoons about life in the Navy, a crossword puzzle, and often a "cheesecake" photograph of a Hollywood starlet. A section written by the WAVES was called "Splashes from the WAVES." A special series for the WAVES to be able to express their ideas and opinions was called "Chats with WAVES." (Courtesy of Florida Historical Society.)

18

Two

A Joint Long-Range Proving Ground

Following World War II, captured German V2 missiles were brought to the United States for study and were subsequently launched from White Sands Proving Ground, New Mexico. When one of these missiles crashed near a cemetery south of Juarez, Mexico, a new area was required to safely conduct future launches of missiles that were increasing in size and flight distance.

In October 1946, the Joint Research and Development Board formed a committee to study possible locations of a joint long-range proving ground for development of guided missiles by all branches of the military. The committee considered numerous sites, but settled on three primary locations: the state of Washington (with a range along the Aleutian Islands); El Centro, California (with a range down the coast of Baja California in Mexico); and the BRNAS in Florida (with launching sites at Cape Canaveral and a range over the Bahama Islands). The Aleutians range was quickly rejected as being too cold, remote, and difficult to support. The committee selected El Centro as its first choice, and Cape Canaveral as its second.

The California range was abandoned as an option after Mexico's president refused to allow missile flights over Baja. The British, on the other hand, were willing to allow missile flights near the Bahamas and agreed to lease land for construction of tracking stations. The Cape Canaveral site, approved in 1947, was far from heavily populated areas, yet accessible by road, waterway, and railway transportation. The former BRNAS, located only 15 miles away, would make an excellent support base.

On May 11, 1949, Public Law 60 was signed by Pres. Harry S. Truman to establish the Joint Long-Range Proving Ground (JLRPG) for guided missile testing. The law authorized $75 million for construction of essential facilities at Cape Canaveral. In October 1949, the JLRPG was activated as a joint undertaking by the Army, Navy, and Air Force. The Air Force was given sole responsibility of the JLRPG in May 1950, and the name changed to Long-Range Proving Ground Base (LRPGB).

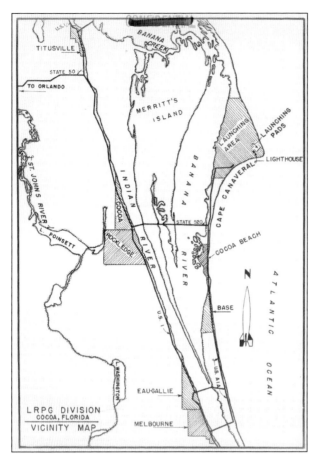

LRPG DIVISION
COCOA, FLORIDA
VICINITY MAP

This map shows the relationship of the headquarters of the LRPGB, located at BRNAS south of Cocoa Beach, and the launch area 15 miles to the north at Cape Canaveral. Numerous name changes to these two facilities through the years have led to much confusion and inaccurate descriptions. This confusion was compounded in 1963 when the City of Cape Canaveral was incorporated just south of the launch area.

The names and name changes of the various entities involved with the LRPG over the years still leads to great confusion. The base was named JLPGB in June 1949; it was changed to just Long-Range Proving Ground Base in May 1950. On August 1, 1950, it was renamed Patrick AFB.

B-1—Joint Long Range Proving Grounds,
Banana River, Fla.
"The Guided Missile Base"

The Advanced Headquarters JLRPG and the Air Force Division JLRPG were established in October 1949 as two separate command groups. The Air Force Division JLRPG was redesignated Long-Range Proving Ground Division (LRPGD) in May 1950. Here, members of the LRPGD's general board attend a meeting.

The LRPGD received approval of its emblem in March 1951. To highlight the division's mission, the shield had a blue background to represent the stratosphere and a silver missile with yellow-and-red flaming exhaust that symbolized a guided missile. In May 1951, the LRPGD was designated a separate operating agency and assigned to Air Research and Development Command (ARDC), making it the equivalent of a numbered Air Force.

This sign on the beach at the Cape Canaveral launch area warned that it was a military facility with restricted access. Similar signs were posted to warn anyone approaching from other directions on foot, by vehicle, or boat. The launch area contained about 25 miles of shoreline before meeting the section known today as Canaveral National Seashore.

The first rocket launch from the Cape Canaveral launch area occurred on July 24, 1950, when Bumper 8 lifted off from Launch Complex 3. Bumper 8 was a German V-2 missile captured toward the end of World War II. It was fitted with a smaller Army rocket known as a WAC Corporal, which served as the second stage. Some sources define WAC as standing for "without attitude control." (Courtesy of Al Hartmann.)

Mason Mathews Patrick was born December 13, 1863, in Lewisburg, West Virginia. He was admitted to the US Military Academy at West Point and graduated second in his class in 1886. He championed giving the Air Service limited autonomy, and in 1926, the new Air Corps was formed. Due in part to Patrick's early efforts, the US Air Force became a separate branch of the military in 1947.

At age 60, Major General Patrick flew the same aircraft as the men in his command. He is pictured here at the controls of his personal aircraft as chief of the Air Service in 1923, the same year he appeared on the cover of *Time* magazine. On August 1, 1950, nearly nine years following his death, a facility in Florida supporting missile testing was named Patrick AFB.

CHIEF OF AIR SERVICE.

PATRICK AIR FORCE BASE

UNITED STATES AIR FORCE
LONG RANGE PROVING GROUND

MAIN BASE
Flight test facility
for guided missiles
of the Army,
Navy & Air Force.

As stated on this vintage postcard, JLRPG served as a missile testing facility for the Army, Navy, and Air Force. The main base for the JLRPG was at Patrick AFB, with much of the testing conducted at the nearby Cape Canaveral launch area. (Author's collection.)

Col. A.J. Bird, base commander from July 28, 1950, to August 19, 1951, addresses attendees at the ceremony that renamed the base in honor of Major General Patrick. Colonel Bird replaced Col. Othel R. Deering, commander of the JLRPGB, the name of the base prior to Patrick AFB. The base was named Patrick AFB on August 1, 1950, but not dedicated until August 26.

The primary mission of Patrick AFB is to support missile testing and launching rockets into space. Along with this responsibility was the requirement to train military, civilian, and contractor personnel in areas including celestial navigation, determining launch and reentry trajectories, orbital mechanics, and hypersonic flight dynamics. Shown here are a teacher and student discussing the celestial coordinate system, learning about right ascension, declination, and the celestial sphere concept. Perhaps to prove that such work really was rocket science, a guided missile school for all personnel of the 4800th Guided Missile Wing was established at Patrick AFB in January 1951. Individuals assigned to the wing were required to attend classes at least one hour daily, five days a week. The 4800th Guided Missile Wing was activated in December 1950 and was involved with testing the Lark missile at the Cape Canaveral launch area.

Pictured in 1951, communication cables are being laid between Patrick AFB and Cape Canaveral's launch area 15 miles to the north by base communications personnel. While rocket and missile testing was being conducted at Cape Canaveral, military and contractor personnel at Patrick AFB needed a reliable way to stay in contact with their representatives.

Housed in Building No. 989 at Patrick AFB, electronics shop personnel were always busy with repairs. Additionally, they built new components to keep the hardware associated with flying airplanes and launching missiles functional. From test equipment to instrumentation necessary to operate a missile testing range, an abundance of work kept these skilled technicians occupied.

The Air Force Missile Test Center (AFMTC) at Patrick AFB refers to all facilities supporting the missile range. AFMTC was part of ARDC. Headquartered in Baltimore, Maryland, ARDC had 10 research, development, and testing centers across the United States. This sign was outside one of the entry gates to Patrick AFB in the early 1950s.

The facilities that supported rocket launches have been known by many names, including Cape Canaveral Auxiliary Air Force Base, Cape Canaveral Test Annex, Cape Canaveral Air Station, Cape Kennedy Air Force Station, or simply "the Cape." Today, rockets fly from CCAFS, not to be confused with the nearby city of Cape Canaveral.

Once operated by ARDC, AFMTC later became an operational component of Air Force Systems Command. AFMTC did not build guided missiles or launch armed missiles; rather, it supported all military and contractors conducting tests at Patrick AFB or the Cape Canaveral launch area.

Air Force Eastern Test Range (AFETR) replaced the AFMTC, and though the name changed, the overall mission remained the same. AFETR's role was to maintain and operate the launch range and all its supporting facilities. Its purpose was to conduct tests and collect data on guided missile and rocket launches. Building No. 423 at Patrick AFB served as headquarters for the AFETR.

Three

AIR OPERATIONS, AIRCRAFT, AND WINGED MISSILES

Patrick AFB had everything one would expect to see at any Air Force facility, like airplanes, helicopters, runways, and hangars. But during the 1950s, Patrick AFB had some things that were not found at most other bases, like winged missiles. Many of the early missiles being tested at the Cape Canaveral launch area were winged missiles, also called cruise missiles or pilotless bombers. Some of these missiles, such as the Snark, were first flown into Patrick AFB aboard large cargo aircraft for inspection and testing before being trucked 15 miles north to the launch area. Later, missiles were flown aboard aircraft directly to the launch area by landing at the nearby Skid Strip, delivered by sea via Port Canaveral, or trucked in overland.

Numerous types of aircraft, prop driven and jet, have flown into and out of Patrick AFB. Some aircraft brought in supplies, soldiers returning home from deployments, visiting presidents, and international dignitaries. Departing aircraft hauled material and personnel to remote downrange tracking stations and other destinations around the world. Aircraft were flown in times of potential conflict such as during the Cuban Missile Crisis. However, most flew during peaceful times with missions of search and rescue and flight crew training. Some specially modified aircraft flew to observe and track missiles launched from the nearby Cape Canaveral launch area.

Winged missiles in the 1950s flew low and relatively slow to their target, and were vulnerable to interception by enemies, but they served a purpose until replaced by ballistic missiles. Vehicles such as the Matador, Mace, Snark, Bomarc, Bull Goose, X-10, and Navaho were flight tested at the Cape Canaveral launch area. With the exception of the X-10, all of the winged missiles used a rocket motor to lift them off the ground before their onboard air-breathing engines took over.

Whether props, rotary blades, or jet engines, Patrick AFB functions like any other Air Force base. Regardless of whether it's a takeoff or a blastoff, air operations at Patrick AFB have always involved functioning as a military airfield as well as overseeing operations at the nearby spaceport.

Construction of Hangar No. 800 began in September 1944. Personnel working on Project Baker moved in during June 1945. Alterations and additions to the hangar occurred through the years. Later, it served as the air terminal for Patrick AFB, supporting transportation of personnel and cargo to downrange tracking stations. The structure was demolished in 2003.

With an elevation of just nine feet above sea level, Patrick AFB is indeed a base built adjacent to the Atlantic Ocean. Aircraft approaching or leaving the base often fly over the beach and Highway A1A, giving those on the sand or driving along in their cars an impromptu air show. Signs along the road warning of low-flying aircraft are posted for a good reason.

In the early 1950s, Matador missiles were delivered in sections by enclosed trucks to Patrick AFB. They were unloaded and placed on flatbed trucks for transport to Building No. 312 for assembly and inspection. By 1953, when construction of Hangars A and B was completed, they were also used in support of Matador and other missiles.

Flight testing of Matador missiles was conducted at Cape Canaveral's launch area, but prior to those tests, the missiles' General Electric Allison J33 engine and other components were tested at Patrick AFB. Following transport to the launch area, the wings were attached, along with a solid-fueled rocket motor under the tail, which was used to get the missile off the ground.

Following initial testing of the Air Force Snark missile at Holloman Air Force Base in New Mexico, testing was moved to Cape Canaveral. At the Cape, three test launches of a dummy, or simulated Snark vehicle, with no wings or tail section, were conducted to test a new zero-length launcher in late 1952. Here, a dummy vehicle is unloaded from a C-124 transport aircraft at Patrick AFB.

Personnel from the AFMTC watch as a Snark missile is unloaded from a C-124 aircraft at Patrick AFB. Snark missiles arrived at the base for inspection prior to being transported on Highway A1A to the Cape Canaveral launching area. Snark was a surface-to-surface cruise missile, with a 5,000-mile range.

A Matador cruise missile sits covered in front of Hangars A and B at Patrick AFB. Matadors and other missiles were initially checked out in these hangars before being moved to the launch area. The two hangars at Patrick AFB, and a third similar structure, Hangar C at the Cape Canaveral launch area, were constructed by the J.H. Sapp Company.

Maj. Reet P. Smith, base operations officer at Patrick AFB, greets Capt. Karl W. Edmundson, operations officer from Dobbins AFB, Georgia, as he arrives with a rare serum to treat a victim of a black widow spider bite. Black widow spiders are just one of many dangerous and venomous creatures found at Patrick AFB and in the surrounding areas.

Technical Sgt. Hardin M. Kurtz (right), of space control and passenger service, discusses an aircraft load plan with Airman First Class Eugene A. Longe at the Patrick AFB Air Terminal. Workers at the terminal included military and civilian air freight and passenger service specialists and enlisted load masters, all working around the clock to keep aircraft on time for their flights. Personnel planned aircraft loads to accommodate transport of passengers and cargo.

Checking that the straps of a pallet of cargo are secure before it is loaded aboard a C-141 Starlifter aircraft are air freight specialists, from left to right, Robert L. Hill, Frederico S. Hortillosa, and Henry T. Farris. The Military Airlift Command provided regularly scheduled flights of cargo and personnel between Patrick AFB and downrange sites such as Pretoria in the Republic of South Africa, approximately 7,100 nautical miles away.

Pictured is the late 1952 arrival at Patrick AFB of Rep. Porter Hardy Jr. and members of a congressional committee. Hardy, a Democrat, was the representative for Virginia's second congressional district from 1947 to 1968. After his political career, he became the director of Dominion Bankshares Corporation and several other financial institutions in Virginia.

This modified version of the Boeing B-17 Flying Fortress heavy bomber was stationed at Patrick AFB beginning in 1952 in support of AFMTC operations. These aircraft, equipped with loudspeakers and VHF radios, were used to warn boats and other planes to stay clear of an area prior to a missile launch. The aircraft remained on duty at Patrick AFB until 1958.

Patrick AFB was one of several bases that conducted research flights as part of Project Jet Stream in 1954. The project was a study of fast-moving air currents at high altitudes, conducted jointly by the Air Force and Navy. The goal was to determine the potential dangers the winds posed for military and commercial pilots, in addition to the feasibility of taking advantage of such high tailwinds.

The 6520th Flight Test Squadron used a B-29 to probe the invisible river of air in the atmosphere racing along at speeds up to 300 miles per hour. Each of the aircraft involved in Project Jet Stream was equipped with instruments to measure wind speed, temperature, turbulence, and humidity.

Fast-moving winds of the jet stream can either make an aircraft nearly stand still if it is flying against the stream or push it along at speeds that can double its range. Turbulence associated with the stream can affect a pilot's ability to control the aircraft and can even throw a rocket off its flight path. Data from Project Jet Stream has made it safer to fly at high altitudes.

In addition to instruments carried aloft to study the jet stream, pilots and other observers aboard the aircraft also recorded their own observations prior to and after encountering the winds. The goal of these visual observations was to discover what to "look for" in hopes of predicting when the dangerous winds of the jet stream would be encountered.

Sitting near Hangar B at Patrick AFB in early 1959, this B-57B aircraft had the nose of a Boeing Bomarc missile grafted onto its forward section. This configuration allowed instruments and sensors to be tested inside under flight conditions. Tests utilizing the aircraft were cheaper and more controlled than those conducted by launching an actual missile, which could not be recovered for study or reuse.

Perhaps wishing for a bit of luck for the testing of Bomarc missile components attached to the nose of this B-57B at Patrick AFB, someone applied a white sticker that reads, "Made in Las Vegas from old slot machine parts." The Bomarc missile system did go on to be a very successful surface-to-air program.

This September 1965 photograph shows Lt. Col. W.D. Baxter briefing two bioastronautics nurses, Capt. Dorothy R. Novotny (left) and Capt. Nancy J. Barron (right), on an emergency rescue via a helicopter. For manned missions into space, especially during the 1960s and early 1970s, Sikorsky CH-30 helicopters were used for recovery of the astronauts at the end of their flights and, in case of an emergency, during launches. Subsequent decades saw the use of other types of helicopters. Bioastronautics is a branch of medicine that deals with exposing living creatures, human and animal, to the rigors and conditions of flights to extreme high altitudes and into space. The field includes the study of chemistry, biology, medicine, and psychology. Bioastronautics also encompasses aspects of pilot and astronaut training, as well as design and development of life-support systems.

Pre-detected telemetry was recorded for the first time on an Air Force aircraft. Those responsible for the accomplishment at Patrick AFB are, from left to right, Herbert Foster, Charles A. Hoppe, E.S. Sanford, Bobby R. Dorton, Ralph E. Robb Jr., Robert D. Reneau, R. Lombardo, Ronald H. Vought, Leonard C. Fyler, and Earl N. Cook. Not pictured are Ward E. Wickham and Jack F. Snider.

A Modified KC-135, designated NKC-135A, was used in the Terminal Radiation Airborne Program (TRAP). Instruments on the aircraft took measurements of radiation effects, and photographs of reentry bodies (nose cones) returning into the atmosphere. TRAP tests were conducted primarily at Patrick AFB and Vandenberg AFB, California.

The numerous round observation ports of this NKC-135 resembled holes in a musical instrument, which explained why it was referred to as a "piccolo tube." This type of aircraft was also known as an Airborne Astrographic Camera System (AACS) and was used to photograph reentry vehicles from ballistic flight. Two AACS aircraft were stationed at Patrick AFB.

This interior view of the NKC-135A aircraft shows high-speed, high-resolution cameras mounted near each of the observation ports. The aircraft was approximately 136 feet long, with a wingspan of 130 feet, and operated at a ceiling of up to 50,000 feet. This photograph was taken between July 1969 and June 1970 at Patrick AFB.

The Airborne Lightweight Optical Tracking System (A-LOTS), built by Northrop Corporation, was a precision photographic system. It provided engineering surveillance photography of missiles and space vehicles during early launch, stage separation, and reentry phases of flight. Located in a pod attached externally to a C-135 aircraft, a 200-inch focal length lens gave the system the ability to photograph and resolve a 12-foot target at a distance of 200 miles.

Staff Sgt. James H. Zocchi inspects a camera in the pod of a C-135 jet aircraft at Patrick AFB that carried the A-LOTS. Sergeant Zocchi was a photographer assigned to the A-LOTS and was making final preparations so the system was ready to film the liftoff of the Apollo 8 mission, the first manned flight to orbit the Moon, in December 1968.

A potential target for tracking by the A-LOTS was first visually spotted by an observer using a B-50-type gunsight through a clear astrodome on top of the aircraft's fuselage, as shown here. An image from these instruments appeared on the screens at the operation console. Adjustments were then made so the object could be tracked either automatically or manually to obtain the best results.

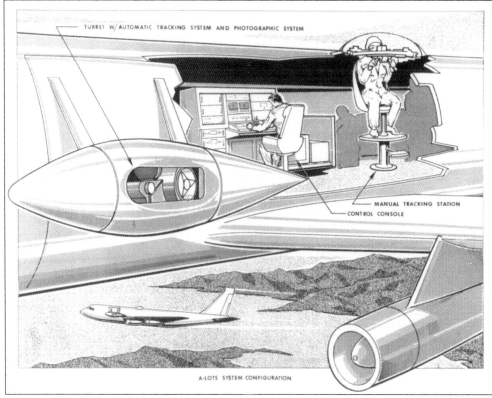

This graphic illustrates the location and relation of components within a C-135 aircraft outfitted with the A-LOTS. Shown are the elevated manual tracking station where an observer sat, the control console where other personnel were stationed, and the large instrumentation pod mounted on the exterior of the aircraft, which housed an optic sensor and a high-speed film camera.

This Lockheed U-2 high-altitude reconnaissance aircraft flew a variety of missions from Patrick AFB, including flights during the Cuban Missile Crisis in 1962. In 1989, a U-2 belonging to the 9th Reconnaissance Wing photographed the launch of a Space Shuttle to aid in identifying any damage that might have occurred early in its flight. (Courtesy of John Hilliard.)

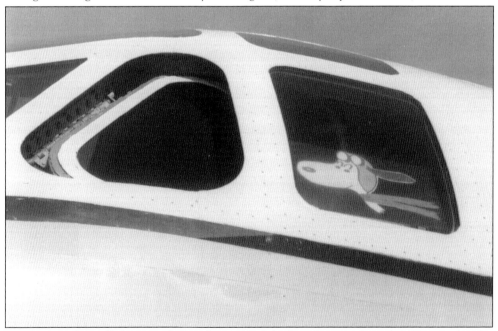

Snoopy was often called upon to help "pilot" a T-39 Sabreliner between Patrick AFB and other Air Force bases throughout the United States. Based on the North American Aviation Sabreliner, this twin-jet, multipurpose aircraft was designated the T-39 by the Air Force and Navy. The aircraft's name reflected its close resemblance to the F-86 Sabre Jet and F-100 Super Sabre.

Astronauts Col. David R. Scott (front seat) and Maj. Alfred M. Worden were greeted at Patrick AFB by aircraft mechanics of the 6549th Organizational Maintenance Squadron's Transient Alert Section. The two astronauts were en route to fly the short distance north to the Kennedy Space Center as soon as Lowell Honeycutt (left) and Ivery Sparks completed an inspection of their T-38 jet.

The Aero Spacelines "Super Guppy" was a large, wide-bodied aircraft used to transport oversized cargo such as rocket components. The Super Guppy was the successor to the "Pregnant Guppy," another aircraft for hauling large payloads. This Super Guppy landed at Patrick AFB on Memorial Day weekend in 1976 to participate in the 3rd Century America Exposition activities.

During the Apollo space program to land men on the Moon, the flight line at Patrick AFB hosted a special type of aircraft known as Apollo Range Instrumentation Aircraft (ARIA). These modified Boeing KC-135 aircraft carried a variety of instrumentation for tracking and receiving telemetry data. Following the Apollo Program, the acronym stayed the same, but the word "Apollo" was changed to "Advanced" as ARIA also supported various military missions.

ARIA aircraft supplemented ships at sea and land-based tracking stations. Together, they created a worldwide communications network with Apollo astronauts in space. ARIA provided two-way voice relay between the Apollo spacecraft and Mission Control Center, in Houston, Texas. ARIA also received telemetry signals from the spacecraft while it was in Earth's orbit and en route to and from the Moon.

ARIA were deployed from Patrick AFB within seven days prior to launch. This schedule allowed for arrival at predetermined locations near the data collect area, with a few days to spare to address any required maintenance or testing. ARIA left their waiting locations with enough time to reach the proper place to perform their mission.

In addition to ARIA, the range also had Telemetry Range Instrumented Aircraft (TRIA) that were similar but did not have the specialized equipment unique to the Apollo program. ARIA and TRIA had "droop snoot" bulbous noses, which, in the case of ARIA, housed a seven-foot parabolic dish antenna for telemetry and communication reception. The nose of TRIA housed two drum-style antennas and the aircraft's radar.

The turboprop driven OV-10 Bronco aircraft flew missions for the Air Force and Marine Corps. It could carry up to three tons of munitions and remain over the target area for several hours. The Department of State based some of its OV-10 aircraft at Patrick AFB when they were not deployed in support of drug interdiction or other missions around the world.

Presidential aircraft, including *Air Force One* and the *Marine One* helicopter, have flown in and out of Patrick AFB numerous times. Several presidents have flown into Patrick AFB or landed at the Skid Strip at the Cape Canaveral launch area, as well as the three-mile long runway at nearby Kennedy Space Center.

A Coast Guard search and rescue helicopter landed at Patrick AFB to deliver a patient in need of emergency medical treatment. The Coast Guard and Air Force Rescue Wings, along with Rescue Squadrons assigned to those wings, continue to fly lifesaving search and rescue missions as needed from Patrick AFB.

CH-3C helicopters were used at Patrick AFB and the Cape Canaveral launch area for numerous tasks. They were an integral part of manned launches in the role of recovery and transport for medical care if necessary. Another important duty was to ferry a range safety officer (RSO) to the area where the Navy was launching a missile from a submarine; if the missile went awry, the RSO would send a destruct signal.

Various models of Sikorsky helicopters were used during the early years of the manned space program to recover space capsules and their crews. Teams practiced standard and emergency procedures using mock-ups of capsules known as "boilerplates." This boilerplate of a three-man Apollo capsule continues to be proudly displayed at Patrick AFB. (Author's collection.)

An HH-53C Super Jolly Green Giant helicopter from the 44th Aerospace Rescue and Recovery Squadron was stationed at Patrick AFB in the early 1970s. It was once used to transport an 8,000-pound radar antenna, which was removed from an Apollo Range Instrumentation Ship, the USNS *Redstone*. The antenna was declared surplus and taken to Patrick AFB where it could be utilized.

Pictured here is a helicopter from Patrick AFB carrying the Experimental Reentry Vehicle (XRV), during filming of scenes for the movie *Marooned*. The XRV was a prop for the movie, which premiered in late 1969, just a few months after the first manned landing on the Moon. Based on a 1964 novel by Martin Caidin, *Marooned* is about three astronauts in orbit who are unable to return home when the retro rocket on their capsule fails to fire. With the astronauts in space running out of air, a daring rescue mission using the XRV is hastily planned. A hurricane threatens to foil the launch from what was then called Cape Kennedy. At the last minute, the eye of the storm moves over the launch pad and the mighty Air Force Titan IIIC rocket sends the rescue craft into space. *Marooned* starred Gregory Peck, Richard Crenna, David Janssen, James Franciscus, Gene Hackman, Lee Grant, Nancy Kovack, and Mariette Hartley. The movie won an Academy Award for its visual effects.

From the Spanish word "killing," the Matador surface-to-surface cruise missile is more accurately defined as a pilotless bomber. It was envisioned as a way of delivering a heavy weapons payload a long distance without endangering a manned crew. Over 280 Matador missiles were tested at the Cape Canaveral launch area.

The Mace was an advanced version of the Matador missile. Mace had a lengthened fuselage to carry more fuel for a greater range, could carry a heavier warhead, and incorporated an improved guidance system. A total of 44 Mace missile launches were conducted at Cape Canaveral.

Classified as a ground-launched cruise missile, the Snark was essentially a pilotless aircraft. A Snark squadron was activated at Patrick AFB in December 1957; it was the first operational long-range guided missile squadron. With a range of more than 5,000 miles, Snark was considered an intercontinental guided missile. Note the serpentine creature painted on the nose. (Courtesy of Al Hartmann.)

Aircraft such as this F-89 served as chase planes to follow Snark missiles downrange after launch. Some Snarks were fitted with retractable landing gear, which allowed for recovery and reuse. Numerous Snarks attempted to return to a landing facility at the Cape Canaveral launch area. Because the Snark had landing skids instead of wheels, the runway was called the Skid Strip, the name it is known by today.

The Air Force Bomarc missile was developed by the Boeing Company and the University of Michigan Aeronautical Research Center, whose initials formed its name. Part of continental air defense, Bomarcs protected the United States from enemy bombers and cruise missiles. Following testing at the Cape Canaveral launch area, Bomarcs were deployed at six American and two Canadian sites during the 1960s but were phased out in 1972.

In the early 1950s, the Air Force and the Fairchild Company studied the concept of a ground-launched long-range decoy missile that could simulate a large strategic bomber on enemy radar. The decoy missile became known as the Bull Goose. Its first test flight at the Atlantic Missile Range (AMR) occurred in June 1957. (Courtesy of Al Hartmann.)

The X-10 research aircraft was basically an unmanned high-performance jet, powered by two turbojet engines and with retractable landing gear. Capable of speeds of nearly Mach 2, the X-10 could have been utilized as an intermediate-range supersonic cruise missile. At Cape Canaveral's launch area, the X-10 served as a test bed for the development of the Navaho, which involved attaching the winged vehicle to a rocket booster.

A modified X-10 aircraft was attached to a liquid-fuel rocket booster to create a new vehicle known as Navaho. Intended to be a supersonic intercontinental cruise missile, Navaho launched vertically. At around 50,000 feet, the two vehicles separated and the winged vehicle's ramjets powered the Navaho farther. Navaho was tested at Launch Complex 9 at CCAFS in 1956 to 1958; however, it was never operationally deployed.

Four "Skybolt" missiles were attached under the wing of a B-52 aircraft during a flight utilizing the AMR. Six Skybolt air-launched ballistic missiles were tested using the AMR operated from Patrick AFB. These missiles were launched from B-52 aircraft having taken off from other bases before flying over the range and firing the missiles downrange. The first of these tests occurred on April 19, 1962.

Hound Dog was a supersonic, air-to-ground missile carried under the wing of B-52 bomber aircraft. At Patrick AFB, Hound Dog missiles were tested from aircraft flying over the AMR, where they were launched and allowed to fly downrange over the Atlantic Ocean. Information gathered from instruments along the range permitted evaluation of the missiles' performance in flight.

Four

ISLAND HOPPING AND SUPPORTING DOWNRANGE

The term "downrange" refers to the general easterly to southeasterly direction that missiles and space vehicles fly following liftoff from the Cape Canaveral launch area. Downrange also refers to the chain of islands where tracking stations were built to follow and receive telemetry signals from vehicles in flight. The overall area of these islands, as well as a vast expanse of ocean within the flight path of launches from the Cape, has been called the Bahamas Long-Range Proving Ground, Atlantic Missile Range, Eastern Test Range, and, since 1990, simply the Eastern Range. It has even been referred to as Cape Canaveral's shooting gallery.

During the 1950s, the range consisted of nine primary tracking sites located over a distance of 1,000 miles: Cape Canaveral, Florida; Jupiter, Florida; and the islands of Grand Bahama, Eleuthera, San Salvador, Mayaguana, Grand Turk, Dominican Republic, and Puerto Rico. By early 1960, the range extended more than 5,000 miles with 13 major sites adding Antigua, St. Lucia, Fernando de Noronha, and Ascension islands. The range was later extended to more than 10,000 miles through the South Atlantic and into the Indian Ocean, where it meets the Western Range, which supports launches from Vandenberg AFB, California. All but the station on Ascension Island have been replaced by more modern methods of tracking a vehicle in flight such as the use of satellites.

A major function of Patrick AFB during buildup of the downrange facilities was transportation of military and civilian contractor personnel, along with equipment and supplies required at the remote sites. Oceangoing ships as well as a variety of aircraft made trips downrange, often "hopping" or stopping at several islands before returning to Florida.

Communication between the islands and facilities in Florida was accomplished by radio and by means of a submarine communications cable. A 1,370-nautical-mile section of submerged cable linking the Cape Canaveral launch area to Puerto Rico was laid in mid-1954, with submarine cable repeater stations installed at Grand Turk and other sites later that year. The cable provided an instant and secure way of sending data.

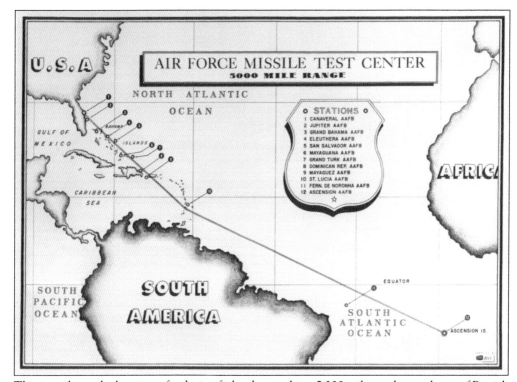

AIR FORCE MISSILE TEST CENTER
5000 MILE RANGE

U.S.A

NORTH ATLANTIC OCEAN

GULF OF MEXICO

BAHAMA
ISLANDS

CARIBBEAN SEA

SOUTH PACIFIC OCEAN

SOUTH AMERICA

AFRICA

EQUATOR

SOUTH ATLANTIC OCEAN

ASCENSION IS.

◦ STATIONS ◦
1 CANAVERAL AAFB
2 JUPITER AAFB
3 GRAND BAHAMA AAFB
4 ELEUTHERA AAFB
5 SAN SALVADOR AAFB
6 MAYAGUANA AAFB
7 GRAND TURK AAFB
8 DOMINICAN REP. AAFB
9 MAYAGUEZ AAFB
10 ST. LUCIA AAFB
11 FERN. DE NORONHA AAFB
12 ASCENSION AAFB

This map shows the location of a chain of islands stretching 5,000 miles to the southeast of Patrick AFB where tracking stations were built. Telemetry antennas and equipment used for tracking rockets in flight were constructed on these islands. The availability of the islands was a major consideration in the selection of the east coast of Florida for launching rockets.

When a missile in flight was over an area that was out of range between islands, ships and aircraft filled the voids. Tracking ships with large dish antennas and modified aircraft with specialized instrumentation followed a missile's progress until it was again picked up by one of the ground-based stations downrange.

For many years, a cannon sat in front of the Downrange Affairs Office at Patrick AFB. The cannon, found on Grand Turk Island, is believed to date from the mid-1600s. The antique piece was displayed at the base to represent Patrick's ties with the many downrange islands. In 1967, it was moved to the Air Force Space & Missile Museum at the Cape Canaveral launch area.

On April 13, 1950, Sir George R. Sandford, governor general of the Bahamas (second from right), was greeted by Brig. Gen. William L. Richardson, commanding general of the LRPGD, and members of the Honor Guard. Cooperation by the Bahamian government was essential for establishment of tracking stations on the downrange islands, as well as permission to fly missiles near those islands.

A test run was made on August 22, 1952, of the Missilair Line, scheduled to haul cargo and passengers between Patrick AFB and the downrange stations using C-47 and C-54 aircraft. The Military Air Transport Services, part of Military Airlift Command, also carried personnel, mail, and supplies from Patrick AFB using C-124, DC-6, and C-121 aircraft.

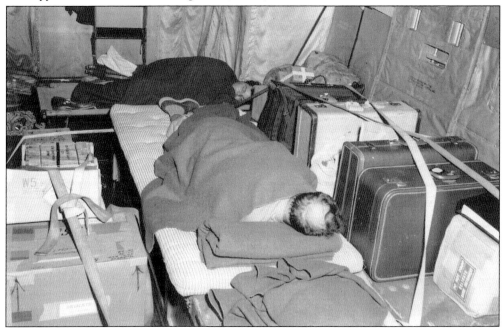

A flight downrange from Patrick AFB to Ascension Island meant traveling more than 5,000 miles with stops along the way. Sleeping accommodations aboard a C-124 transport aircraft were basically anywhere a cot could be set up among all the luggage and cargo also being transported. Here, two men find a comfortable spot during a flight in September 1956.

A Convair C-131 aircraft sits on an airfield of a downrange island in 1958. Compared to Air Force facilities in the United States, the auxiliary Air Force bases on the islands downrange were considered sparse and primitive. Each island base had a military base commander and a civilian base manager.

The first radar site on the island of Ascension was built on the flattened top of a volcano in 1957; other tracking equipment was installed in the years following. Ascension was designated as a "singles only" assignment, meaning that the island was too remote to be conducive to family life. According to this photograph, however, birds seem to be more than welcome at the island.

This is a view of the Ascension Island runway area (upper left), overlooking the parking ramp. Some personnel assigned to Ascension Island were housed at an Air Force base near Wideawake Airfield. A tracking station to support launches of manned Apollo missions to the Moon was built in the mid-1960s on the eastern corner of the island in an area known as the Devil's Ashpit.

The Grumman Albatross was a large twin-engine flying boat used by the Air Force, Navy, and Coast Guard predominately as a search and rescue aircraft. For the Air Force, the Albatross was designated SA-16. At Patrick AFB, this aircraft was used to transport personnel between the base and numerous downrange islands.

Fernando de Noronha is an archipelago consisting of 21 islands; the main island is approximately seven square miles. This 1958 image shows Morro do Pico (Peak Mount), the highest point at more than 1,000 feet. Tracking Station No. 11, approximately 3,500 miles from Patrick AFB, was in use at Fernando de Noronha beginning in 1957.

A technician operates a component of optical tracking equipment with several cameras at the downrange station at Grand Bahama Island. This station was the first of the downrange tracking facilities built beyond Florida.

An outdoor theater was one of very few amenities awaiting personnel assigned to the downrange station at San Salvador. This photograph is dated October 31, 1951; spending Halloween on a 63-square-mile island might be a little scary. San Salvador is famous for being visited and named by the explorer Christopher Columbus in 1492.

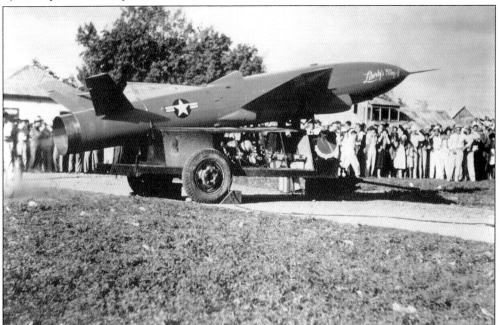

This "simulated missile," named Liberty's Slinger, was a prop taken to some downrange locations to explain the concept of a winged missile. The missile was a way of showing local residents why tracking stations were being built on their home islands. The missile did not fly, but flames shot out the back, and it made a tremendous roar.

The little building with the half moon on the door, labeled "the Sound Box," was one of the Air Force facilities at Savannah Sound on the island of Eleuthera. Tracking Station No. 4 supported the Eastern Test Range from Eleuthera Auxiliary Air Force Base in the 1960s and 1970s.

Even with all the highly sophisticated technology associated with launching missiles and spacecraft, some equipment and facilities downrange were quite primitive. Examples include using tents to house some of the personnel, dirt runways, and this vintage locomotive used to haul supplies.

When the downrange sites were initially constructed, communication between the islands and Patrick AFB was considered critical. In the 1950s, more than 16,000 miles of undersea cable was installed between the various islands. Repairing and splicing undersea cable was a special skill.

Ships used to lay undersea cables were referred to as cable-layers or cable-ships. Ocean conditions and the topography of the sea bottom determined how much cable a ship could install in a day. The cables were specially constructed to survive the pressure and saltwater environment associated with being submerged. Much of the cable was supplied by the Western Electric Company.

Five

TECH LAB AND ROCKETS ON DISPLAY

Construction began in 1954 on the Air Force Technical Laboratory, or "Tech Lab," located at Patrick AFB, which soon became a vital launch support facility. Data from radar tracking devices, telemetry signals from vehicles in flight received at ground stations, and film from cameras recording launches were all processed at the Tech Lab to produce a Flight Test Report. The report allowed engineers a look at every event to evaluate and determine the degree of success of each flight. Missile and space launch systems were tested and perfected in the fewest number of flights due to personnel who worked in this facility, the ground-based and airborne data gathering instruments, and those who evaluated the data.

In 1972, Air Force Technical Applications Center (AFTAC) headquarters was moved from Virginia to part of the Tech Lab building at Patrick AFB. AFTAC is responsible for monitoring and detecting nuclear events anywhere in the world. Whether underground, underwater, in the atmosphere, or in space, AFTAC's detection mission is closely linked to its nuclear treaty monitoring mission. AFTAC monitors compliance with the 1963 Limited Test Ban Treaty, as well as other agreements throughout the world. The 1963 treaty allows nuclear testing only underground, and prohibits the release of nuclear debris or radiation from such tests into the atmosphere outside the national borders of the country performing the tests. Though much of the Tech Lab building was demolished in 2015, a new facility now houses AFTAC, allowing its important national security mission to continue.

Between 1956 and 1996, the Tech Lab was a tourist destination for those wanting to see missiles and space launch vehicles up close. Nine different vehicles have stood on display between the Tech Lab and Highway A1A. The iconic scene of winged missiles and towering rockets in a row, with the Tech Lab as a majestic backdrop, has been captured on numerous postcards and countless visitor snapshots and home movies. In 1976, during the nation's bicentennial celebration, a time capsule to be opened in 2075 during the US tricentennial was placed in a concrete vault in front of the Tech Lab.

Inside the Tech Lab were various electronic devices, early computers, and many highly skilled personnel required to compile and analyze data from the world's largest outdoor laboratory: Florida's Atlantic Missile Range. Information from instruments on the ground, in the air, at sea, and from missiles in flight was funneled into the Tech Lab for study.

The Tech Lab at Patrick AFB, Building No. 989, was 1,046 feet long, 240 feet wide, and 79 feet tall. It had 198 rooms and nearly 455,000 square feet of floor space. Its impressive size and high visibility, due to its location along Highway A1A, made the Tech Lab an iconic landmark for anyone driving past. (Courtesy of John Hilliard.)

Soon after World War II, Gen. Dwight Eisenhower ordered procedures to monitor nuclear programs around the world. In 1947, he directed the Army Air Forces to develop methods of detecting atomic explosions anywhere they occurred. From that directive, and after the Air Force was created, the Air Force Technical Applications Center was established. AFTAC assumed responsibility for the Long-Range Detection Program. AFTAC is the Department of Defense agency responsible for monitoring compliance with several international nuclear treaties. AFTAC moved from Virginia to the Tech Lab at Patrick AFB in 1972 and was given three floors of the C-Wing, and one floor of B-Wing, with a total area of about 86,000 square feet. Much of the Tech Lab was demolished in 2015. A new facility for AFTAC, a 276,000-square-foot command and control facility, was completed at Patrick AFB in 2014.

A Matador surface-to-surface cruise missile was the first vehicle placed on display in front of the Tech Lab in August 1956. The men in the photograph offer a good size comparison to the 39.5-foot-long missile with a 28.6-foot wingspan. The Matador was built by the Glenn L. Martin Company.

A Matador missile shines bright in the Florida sun as it sits on its mount in front of the newly constructed Tech Lab at Patrick AFB. At the time of its installation, the missile was said to stand as a symbol of research being conducted at AFMTC. Construction of the Tech Lab was completed in June 1956; the Matador was put on display two months later.

The Atlas Agena space launch vehicle was erected at the Tech Lab in August 1966 and was the last rocket put on display. The Atlas D-1 booster was shipped from Sheppard Air Force Base, Texas, in March 1966, and the Agena segment at the top arrived the same month from a Lockheed facility in Sunnyvale, California. Workers used many of the same tools and techniques to set up the missile display as if they were erecting it at the launch pad in preparation for liftoff. The Atlas Agena combination was an Atlas booster with an Agena upper stage attached to the payload at the top. The job of the upper stage was to propel the payload farther into space, or boost it on course to reach the Moon or planets. The Atlas Agena vehicle was in use from 1961 to 1978.

Prior to being lifted to the vertical position, the Agena segment had to be attached to the Atlas booster section so the two could be lifted as one piece. The Atlas Agena was also used during the manned Gemini program in the mid-1960s to put the Agena upper stage in orbit as a docking target for the Gemini capsule.

Two cranes were needed to lift the first stage of an Air Force Titan I Intercontinental Ballistic Missile (ICBM) onto its display base in front of the Tech Lab. Installation of the Titan I was completed in November 1961. The missile had been on display at the Civic Center in Denver, Colorado, before being brought to Patrick AFB.

Workers look small next to the first stage of a Titan I ICBM being readied for display. The first stage was just over 50 feet tall. The second stage, to the right, was the next piece lifted into place. Between 1959 and 1962, 47 Titan I missiles were tested at the Cape Canaveral launch area.

"Toyland" had some pretty big toys that were taller than the surrounding palm trees. The missiles on display in front of the Tech Lab were identical in size to real missiles, but were either test articles or training aids and were never meant to be flight-worthy. Most of the interior components that would have been found in flight vehicles were removed from those displayed.

The Office of Information at Patrick AFB produced this brochure for the many people visiting the outdoor missile display. In addition to a photograph of the exhibit, and a map with directions to the area, the brochure also states, "Visitors find this display an interesting and impressive representation of America's missile might and well worth seeing. The display lends itself especially well to family photography."

The missile exhibit at Patrick AFB was featured on the cover of a road map for the state of Florida published in October 1963 by the Esso Oil Company. With the beginning of manned spaceflight in the early 1960s, it was a time in the nation's history when many had a fascination for anything pertaining to missiles and launches into space. (Author's collection.)

Nine missiles were on public display in front of the Tech Lab at Patrick AFB from 1956 to 1996. Pictured here are, from left to right, Bomarc, Polaris, Matador, Pershing I, Snark, Thor, Titan I, and Minuteman. Not pictured is the Atlas Agena, which was the last rocket added in 1966.

An August 1965 launch of a Minuteman II missile from Launch Complex 32B at CCAFS streaks through the night sky as seen from 15 miles away at the Patrick AFB Tech Lab. Night launches are a favorite for photographers who try to capture a time-lapse "streak shot" that dramatically shows the path of the rocket from the launch pad to a distance high in the sky.

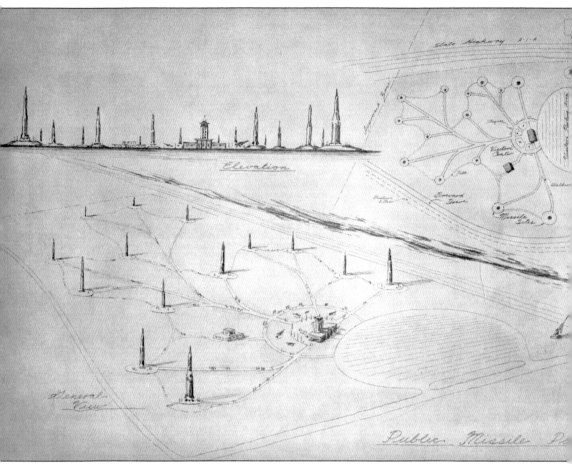

The popularity of the rockets on display in front of the Tech Lab created several safety issues. First, tourists often had to walk across several lanes of busy highway traffic. Second, there was the possibility that the taller missiles could blow over during a hurricane and block the highway. To alleviate these concerns, plans were drawn to move the missile display to an area north of the Tech Lab that would allow for closer parking and would be farther away from the highway. The plan for a new "Rocket Garden" with walkways, a visitors' center, and ample parking, never got beyond the drawing board. Through the years, some of the missiles were indeed damaged by high winds, while others succumbed to deterioration and corrosion due to exposure to the salt air associated with being such a short distance from the ocean. By 1996, the last of the missiles were taken down.

Harry Borst, (right) foreman of the masonry shop, and Staff Sgt. Robert A. Hamilton are placing a stainless steel cask to hold a time capsule into a concrete pedestal. The cask was made by the Aircraft Maintenance Section, the pedestal by the Civil Engineering group, and Transportation Section personnel handled the contents' preservation treatment. The work of packing the contents was delegated to Master Sgt. Art Hicks.

The 29th anniversary of the Air Force (September 18, 1947) and the US bicentennial were marked concurrently on September 18, 1976, at a ceremony in front of the Tech Lab. Brig. Gen. Don M. Hartung, AFETR commander, officiated at the ceremony, which included the dedication of a time capsule to be opened in 2075. Items in the time capsule were supplied by military and community organizations.

In addition to an American and bicentennial flag that flew over Patrick AFB on July 4, 1976, the time capsule contains nearly 100 items considered by Brigadier General Hartung as "intrinsic to an activity that has been significantly involved in an important era of American history, has advanced the cause of freedom throughout the world, and has carried the message of liberty into the far reaches of space." Contents of the time capsule include various newspapers and magazines describing celebrations of the bicentennial; Patrick AFB and Brevard County, Florida, phone directories; booklets detailing the history of Patrick AFB; brochures about the unmanned Viking missions to Mars; and bicentennial sugar packets. A rumor has long circulated around Patrick AFB that a "surprise" item may have been put into the time capsule just before it was sealed. The story goes that someone slipped in a container that, when opened, would release two spring-loaded toy snakes. A note may have been included that reads: "We had a sense of humor in our time. We hope you have one also."

Six

AT WORK AND PLAY

A booklet for newcomers to Patrick AFB in the late 1950s included the statement, "Reporting for duty at the Air Force Eastern Test Range will be the beginning of one of the most unusual tours of your career." Whether working at Patrick or the nearby Cape Canaveral launch area as a military serviceman or a civilian contractor, the booklet goes on to state, "You will know that you are a member of the aerospace team that is building America's deterrent force for tomorrow and forging the conquest of space." The work being done at Patrick AFB and the Cape was unique and vital to the nation; some of it was top secret, and some was front-page news.

The adage of "work hard, play hard" applied to those who were part of Team Patrick. The base offered many activities for those stationed there as well as for family members living with them. A marina, golf course, and various sport venues on base offered a variety of ways to relax and have fun.

A letter by Maj. Gen. Leighton I. Davis, commander, reads, "You will find this a friendly base and a friendly surrounding community." Contractor personnel and servicemen could find numerous things to do in communities near the base. Miles of coastline offered opportunities for surfing, swimming, and time with family at the beach. With the ocean and a river nearby, fishing and water skiing were favorite activities for many. Disney World, which opened in 1971, and other theme parks were only a short drive away.

Of interest to the general public were special events such as air shows that allowed them access to the base. In May 1956, a Matador missile was launched as part of an Armed Forces Day celebration; thousands of local residents were able to see the launch up close as it roared eastward over Highway A1A toward the Atlantic Ocean.

With a few exceptions, the work at Patrick AFB and the Cape was unique. From the flight line to the launch pads, the duty was unusual, as promised.

Yolande Betbeze, Miss America 1951, poses next to the Bluetail Fly missile while visiting Patrick AFB in December 1950. The display belonged to the 3rd Guided Missile Squadron, 550th Guided Missile Wing. Betbeze, a 21-year-old native of Mobile, Alabama, won the Miss America Pageant in September 1950 in Atlantic City, New Jersey.

The Bluetail Fly was an American version of the World War II German V-1 Buzz Bomb known as the JB-2. The missile was often displayed at community events such as this parade during the Orange Festival in Cocoa, Florida, in the early 1950s.

Maj. Gen. Donald N. Yates, AFMTC commander from August 1954 to May 1960, was presented a symbolic key to the Capehart housing area at Patrick AFB in 1958. In August 1955, Congress passed the Capehart Housing Act, which required private developers to build housing units for the military. When the houses were completed, the military set the rental costs.

Preparations are being made for the release of a weather balloon from the weather station at Patrick AFB in 1950. Data including the speed and direction of the winds at various altitudes was invaluable for arriving and departing aircraft. When the balloon burst at high altitude, the tiny instrument package it carried floated back to the ground via the parachute held by the person on the right.

The first public showing of a B-61A Martin Matador missile was in front of thousands of spectators at Patrick AFB during an Armed Forces Day celebration in May 1954. The Matador was the first "pilotless bomber" of the Air Force and was capable of carrying a nuclear or conventional warhead.

Armed Forces Day celebrations provided a rare opportunity for the general public to visit the base and see military aircraft up close. The aircraft taking off in the background is a B-47 Stratojet, the country's first swept-wing multi-engine bomber.

Launch crew members make final preparations to the Florida Ranger, a Matador missile being readied for launch during Armed Forces Day in 1956. An estimated 25,000 people were present to take in the day's festivities and to watch the launch. Launches were usually conducted at the Cape Canaveral launch area and could only be seen from many miles away.

The general public witnessed a launch of a Matador missile as part of Armed Forces Day activities at Patrick AFB on May 20, 1956. This was the first public firing of a Matador missile, and the only missile launch ever conducted at Patrick AFB. Spectators watched as the missile blasted off to the east flying over Highway A1A as it headed out over the ocean. (Courtesy of John Hilliard.)

This young lady checks out the gauges and switches associated with an aircraft's fuel control system during the Armed Forces Day celebration at Patrick AFB on May 16, 1954. Perhaps she was thinking about joining the Air Force when she got a little older.

1st Lt. William L. Richardson Jr., a pilot at Patrick AFB, helps a young visitor try on a flight helmet and oxygen mask. While maybe daydreaming of flying airplanes when they grow up, eager children wait their turn to wear the gear that pilots wear.

Brig. Gen. Don M. Hartung, AFETR commander, displays a Tank Checkout certificate he had just earned. The certificate was presented by Lt. Col. Herbert A. Jordan of the Army Field Office at Patrick AFB. Sgt. Howell W. Ramsey, from the Army Readiness Group, was the training instructor.

Patrick AFB personnel are shown on the firing range during a training course on the proper care and use of the M2 Carbine rifle. The M2 was similar in appearance to the M1 but featured a selector switch that allowed it to fire either semiautomatic or fully automatic.

Of utmost importance to any member of the military, whether at a base in the United States or deployed far from home, was receiving mail. The latest issue of *Time* magazine and letters from family and friends were always welcome. Here, an airman first class assists a captain at the new Patrick AFB Post Office in late 1951.

These four ladies were members of the March of Dimes campaign at Patrick AFB in 1952. The March of Dimes charity was originally called the National Foundation for Infantile Paralysis. It was founded by Pres. Franklin D. Roosevelt in 1938 to fight polio.

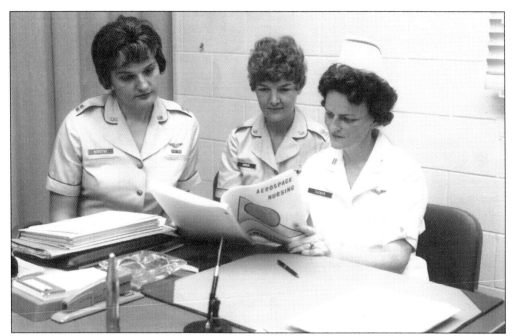

Capt. Pearl E. Tucker (right) discusses the curriculum of an aerospace nursing residency course first taught at Patrick AFB. Capts. Dorothy Novotny (left) and Nancy J. Barron were original members of the Air Force Nurse Corps who participated in the specialized course. They worked with the staff of the bioastronautics section in support of manned space launches and other aerospace medical projects.

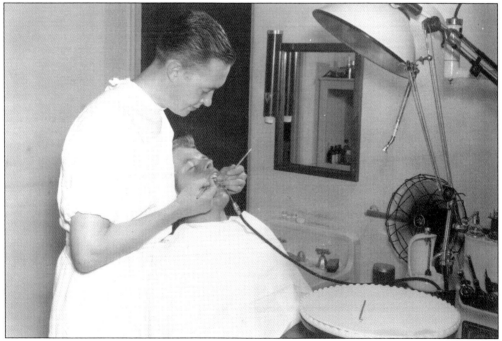

A dental procedure is seen at the medical facilities of Patrick AFB in the early 1950s. Perhaps the nearby fan offered some measure of comfort for the patient in the chair undergoing treatment.

Several baseball and softball fields were established at Patrick AFB though the years. They were often moved for construction of new buildings or additional housing areas. The field pictured here was near the Wherry housing area toward the southern part of the base. In 1949, Sen. Kenneth Wherry of Nebraska introduced a bill that provided for construction of military family housing.

An Air Force technical sergeant was the umpire during a Special Services ballgame at Patrick AFB in 1951. The Patrick AFB team played games against other base personnel, teams from around the community, and against teams from different military bases. Such games fostered feelings of camaraderie and were a nice break from work for players and spectators.

A jump ball began play for this basketball game at Patrick AFB. The sign on the wall reads, "Air Force Eastern Test Range Cape Kennedy," which dates the photograph between 1963 and 1973. The range was renamed Cape Kennedy during this time to honor President Kennedy after he was assassinated.

This March 1952 photograph shows the boxing team at Patrick AFB. As with other sports, boxing was a popular event between teams from other military installations. A winning boxing team was often a source of great pride and bragging rights. One can only wonder if the boxer with the cast on his arm won or lost his previous match.

A Special Services football team is pictured at Patrick AFB during a 1951 game. Note that the helmets only have a thin strap to hold them on, and no one appears to be wearing a face mask or mouthpiece. The base newspaper, the *Missileer*, ran weekly recaps of the results from the intramural league.

Bowling facilities were available at the Comet Bowl-A-Drome in the Airman's Service Club across from the Base Exchange. The bowling alley was operated by the Base Exchange and open to all base personnel and their guests. Today, a new, updated bowling alley is available for those wanting to knock down some pins.

Before modern electric paper shredders, the only way to properly dispose of classified materials was to burn them. This incinerator, referred to as Building No. 963, has a sign that read: "Burn only classified materials here—no trash." Much of the work related to missile testing was classified. Due to the sensitive nature of their work, personnel were instructed to take precautions to maintain the security of classified information and materials. They were told to not carry on conversations about missiles or missile testing except in a closed office and to not ask questions unless there was a need to know the answer. A mid-1950s booklet from the Office of Information states, "Remember, the enemy can learn much from seemingly harmless bits of information. Don't give him the opportunity to learn it from you."

Fuel trucks, such as this one at Patrick AFB in 1951, were used to fuel aircraft, as well as Matador missiles when undergoing tests. The Matador had a J33 turbojet engine, and before it was moved to the Cape Canaveral launch area for a flight test, the missile was thoroughly checked out at Patrick AFB. Part of the checkout procedures required starting and running the engine to verify it was ready for flight.

The Emergency Rescue Squad, part of the Patrick AFB Fire Department, was a three-man crew assigned to Rescue Truck No. 7. The rescue squad's primary mission was to provide first-aid treatment to injured victims of an emergency situation. Rescue Truck No. 7 was painted lime green for maximum visibility and was equipped with many forcible entry tools and first-aid equipment.

A few moments of down time allowed these men to escape into a good book or thumb through the latest magazines. The Patrick AFB Library opened in September 1950. Today, the library offers services unheard of in the 1950s, such as high-speed internet access, movies on Blu Ray, and games for Xbox and PlayStation.

A replica of a two-man Gemini spacecraft nicknamed "Santa-1" was on display near the hospital at Patrick AFB during December 1966. "Reports" indicated that the Eastern Test Range would track "Astronaut Claus" to help him on his journey around the world. The Gemini program carried 10 crews into space between 1965 and 1966, and included the first American space walks and first docking missions.

Maj. Gen. Donald N. Yates was AFMTC commander from August 1954 to May 1960. Here, he reads mail from the public following an NBC television program on which he appeared on December 28, 1958. The documentary, narrated by Chet Huntley, examined the procedures to launch an Atlas rocket. Additionally, the program explained the ability to broadcast a Christmas message to the world from President Eisenhower. The launch on December 18, 1958, put the entire rocket into orbit with a communications payload known as Project SCORE (Signal Communications by Orbiting Relay Equipment). A tape recorder aboard the rocket relayed the following message back to Earth: "This is the President of the United States speaking. Through the marvels of scientific advance, my voice is coming to you from a satellite circling in outer space. My message is a simple one: Through this unique means I convey to you and to all mankind, America's wish for peace on Earth and goodwill toward men everywhere."

A Thor Able rocket lifted off on May 21, 1959, from Launch Complex 17, Cape Canaveral launch area. Tucked in the reentry body, or nose cone, at the top of the rocket was a letter addressed to Maj. Gen. Donald N. Yates, AFMTC commander at Patrick AFB. (Courtesy of John Hilliard.)

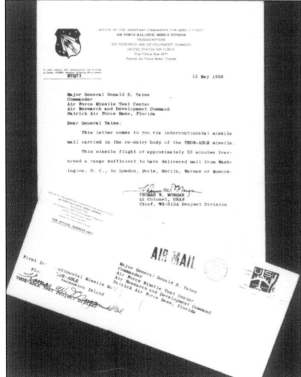

This "rocket mail" took a 33-minute ride into space inside the nose cone of a Thor Able rocket before splashing down in the Atlantic Ocean near Ascension Island. The letter traveled nearly 5,000 miles, the equivalent of a trip from Washington, DC, to Moscow. This was the first piece of intercontinental missile mail.

Building No. 439, constructed in 1945 to serve as the post chapel for BRNAS, continues to fulfill that function as part of Patrick AFB. Chaplains offer confidential counseling and guidance for a wide range of spiritual matters. Opening ceremonies were held in March 1959 for a new educational wing at the chapel.

Chapel No. 2 at Patrick AFB, located in the Capehart housing area, hosted a grand opening ceremony on March 24, 1963. Occupancy was allowed on March 15, 1963, even though the air-conditioning system had not yet been completed. The cost of the chapel was a little more than $298,000.

An issue of the *Missileer* was placed aboard a Titan IIIC rocket prior to launch. Present were, from left to right, John Harris, Martin Company; Maj. Edwin Speaker, chief of Titan III operations; Bob Robinson and Jack Hull, Martin Company; Staff Sgt. Hugh Phillips and Lt. Ray Cauwet, *Missileer* staff; and Lt. Mike Spradlin, Titan III operations.

A Titan IIIC rocket with a copy of the Patrick AFB newspaper aboard lifted off on June 18, 1965, from Launch Complex 40 at Cape Kennedy Air Force Station. This was the first launch of the Titan IIIC, and in addition to the newspaper, it carried a 21,000-pound simulated payload. The newspaper and the payload made it into orbit. (Courtesy of John Hilliard.)

Airman Patricia Piepenbrink arrived at Patrick AFB on March 15, 1976, with Schwartz, an 80-pound German Shepherd. The pair was the first team of handler and military working dog used at Patrick AFB. The initial contingent called for five dogs and their handlers at the base. Once used only as sentry guards and to attack intruders, the role of the military working dog has changed to include tracking, searching, and detection of banned substances. The dogs are not trained to kill; they are taught to be docile and tame unless alerted by their handler. Upon command from the handler, a dog will seize an intruder or suspect by the forearm or leg. If the person does not struggle, the dog will simply hold onto them until told to release. If suspects try to free themselves, or attempt to hurt the dog, it will defend itself by biting.

Staff Sgt. James W. Clifton (left) and Airman First Class Joel M. Cope, of the 6550th Transportation Squadron, hold down an alligator that had invaded the base. The gator was captured by the men when they found it wandering near an active runway. Stray animals were often relocated to avoid posing a danger to personnel or activities around the base.

A military "working cat" is taking a few moments to relax before getting back to its duties of patrolling the hangar in search of mice. This four-legged guard was assigned to the 920th Fuel System Repair Shop at Patrick AFB. The use of cats on military installations as a rodent deterrent was a fairly common practice. (Author's collection.)

In September 1952, a request was made by residents to construct an elementary school at Patrick AFB. Plans were finalized, and construction began in September 1952 for a school that could accommodate up to 420 children in grades one through six. The school opened as a unit of the Florida Public School System in August 1953. In June 1955, the responsibility of operating the school was officially transferred to Patrick AFB.

Children inspect a C-119 military transport aircraft at Patrick AFB in 1953 during National Kids Day. The Fairchild C-119 was also known as the "Flying Boxcar," due mostly to its appearance and partially due to its primary mission. The World War II–era aircraft was designed to carry cargo and personnel, with the ability to drop either by parachute.

Port Canaveral, located on the southern edge of Cape Canaveral's launch area, was officially opened in a dedication ceremony on November 4, 1953. Patrick AFB military and civilian personnel were invited to attend the festivities. The daylong event included tours of several Navy ships docked at the port, free boat tours around the harbor, music from local high school bands, a flag-raising ceremony, a fish-fry lunch, and other activities. Pictured here taking part in the dedication are, from left to right, Captain B.C. McCaffee, commanding officer, Jacksonville Naval Air Station; Maj. Gen. William L. Richardson, commander, AFMTC; and the Hon. Spessard Holland, US senator from Florida and former governor of Florida.

The TPQ-18 (Transportable Special Purpose) radar was a high-precision pulse tracking radar designed specifically to track missiles in flight and objects in space. It provided position and velocity information in real time for evaluation by the RSO. These radar systems were located at Patrick AFB and Merritt Island, Florida, and on the downrange islands of Grand Turk, Antigua, and Ascension.

This 10-turn helix telemetry antenna, being operated by Richard Flamm on top of the Tech Lab, had to be pointed manually at the target to receive signals being transmitted from a missile in flight. Telemetry is data being radioed back to the ground from a transmitter onboard the missile relaying information about the condition of the vehicle. Telemetry signals were recorded for later study and evaluation.

The FPS-16 (Fixed Instrumentation Radar) was a very accurate ground-based single object tracking radar system used by the Air Force and NASA in the late 1950s to early 1960s. The radar used a 12-foot diameter dish and had a positioning accuracy of about seven yards at a distance of up to 500 nautical miles.

These domes housed one search-type and two height finding–type radar systems; the domes protected the equipment from exposure to the elements. The general surveillance radar site at Patrick AFB was a joint operation between the Federal Aviation Administration and the Air Defense Command. The domes and radar were removed in the late 1980s.

Brig. Gen. Harry J. "Bud" Sands Jr., AFMTC vice commander, spoke at a memorial service at Patrick AFB on November 25, 1963, remembering the late president John F. Kennedy. President Kennedy's goal of landing a man on the Moon before the end of the 1960s was a driving force behind the work being accomplished at Patrick AFB and other nearby facilities.

During a televised address to the nation on Thanksgiving Day 1963, Pres. Lyndon Johnson announced that the names of launch facilities in Florida would be changed to honor the late president John F. Kennedy. CCAFS became Cape Kennedy Air Force Station, and the NASA launch area became John F. Kennedy Space Center. In May 1973, the Air Force station reverted back to its original name of Cape Canaveral.

This c. 1961 aerial photograph shows development of the Patrick AFB Yacht Club just south of the runway at top left. In August 1960, the Mason M. Patrick Memorial Trophy was first awarded for competition in a pram regatta, sponsored by the Patrick AFB and Radio Corporation of America Yacht Clubs. The trophy was for skippers under the age of 15 from Brevard County, Florida. (Courtesy of Glenna Holmes.)

This May 1970 view shows the Patrick AFB Yacht Club (foreground) and construction of State Road 404 (upper center). The road, also known at the Pineda Causeway, opened in 1971 as a toll road. The tolls were removed in 1990. The causeway is the nearest east-west highway linking the barrier island that Patrick AFB is on to the mainland. (Courtesy of Glenna Holmes.)

One story is that officers from ARDC teamed up with some Navy officers to construct this "floating contraption" for relaxation purposes. Powered by an outboard motor, the craft spent a lot of time on the Banana River. The flag showing crossed martini glasses may however suggest its primary purpose. (Courtesy of Emily Perry.)

Active-duty servicemen and military veterans have long found recreational opportunities at Patrick AFB. Boating remains a favorite activity for many, whether going out on the Banana River or venturing into the Atlantic Ocean. The Patrick AFB Marina has facilities for mooring, and Recreational Services has boats, kayaks, surfboards, and other water accessories for qualified military personnel to rent. (Courtesy of Glenna Holmes.)

A pontoon boat was popular for taking families out for a day on the Banana River. Whether just motoring around or stopping to fish for redfish, black drum, or anything that takes the bait, the pontoon boat offered a stable platform for large groups, and its roof provided some relief from the Florida sun. This boat and others for use by military personnel was kept at the Boat House at Patrick AFB.

Part of the Air Force fleet at Patrick AFB, this patrol boat served in the waters surrounding the base. The Boat House, visible in the background, was built when the base was known as the BRNAS.

Long before any golfer could tee up a ball for a round at the Patrick AFB Golf Course, much work was needed to turn this swampy area into playable fairways and greens. H.J. Crawford, at upper right, an entomologist at Patrick AFB, is conducting a mosquito larvae count in March 1960.

This vintage postcard shows players enjoying a round of golf at the Patrick AFB course. The first nine holes of the course were opened for play in May 1961, and the course and clubhouse were officially opened in July 1961. Construction of the back nine holes was completed and opened for play in 1965. The course remains a favorite place for active-duty and retired military and civilian duffers today.

The golf course at Patrick AFB was originally designed in the 1950s by world-renowned golf course architect Robert Trent Jones Sr. The 18-hole, par 72 course is known today as the Manatee Cove Golf Course and encompasses more than 200 scenic acres of land, lakes, and river frontage. The course is shared with many animal species, such as manatees, which swim in the water near the first tee box. In 2005, the old clubhouse was replaced with a new 12,000-square-foot facility. In 2007, the Bermuda grass that had been used to form the greens was replaced with Paspallum, a hardier grass that could better withstand the salt-air environment at Patrick AFB. Located near the sixth hole is this Air Force symbol cut into the grass and filled with sand. Each element of the symbol has a special meaning. Overall, the symbol portrays two powerful images, an eagle and a medal of valor. (Courtesy of William Scenna.)

The Air Force Space & Missile Museum is at CCAFS and receives guidance and support from Patrick AFB. In November 1963, members of the command staff at Patrick AFB were appointed to a museum advisory board chaired by Brig. Gen. Harry J. Sands, to provide input for establishing the Air Force Space & Missile Museum at the Cape Canaveral launch area. Several sites were considered until November 1964, when Launch Complex 26 was assigned to the AFMTC's Office of Information for the purpose of a space museum. Launch Complex 26 was the site of the first American satellite (*Explorer I*) launch in 1958. The monkeys Gordo, Able, and Baker were also launched there on their pioneering missions to pave the way for American astronauts. The museum has hosted more than 15 million visitors from around the world since its opening in the late 1960s.

Seven

AIR FORCE MISSILES AND THE MODERN ERA

Ballistic missiles were considered an improvement over the earlier winged missiles because they carry their explosive warheads out of the atmosphere and then reenter and approach the targets from a greater height and speed. Work at Patrick AFB and CCAFS involved perfecting the launch vehicles and testing various types of reentry vehicles, which allowed the warheads to withstand the rigors of reentry.

In parallel with the development of weapons of war were many of the same technologies required for placing scientific satellites and humans into space for peaceful purposes. Rockets being used for military testing were adapted for launching satellites and astronauts. A modified Redstone missile carried the first American satellite into orbit and launched the first American astronauts. The Atlas and Titan II missiles carried astronauts into orbit from 1962 to 1966.

Military rockets were replaced over the years with rockets built with the sole purpose of carrying satellites or humans into space. Vehicles such as the Saturn, the Space Shuttle, variations of the Delta, and modified civilian versions of the Atlas and Titan, along with boosters built by private commercial companies, have been used to launch satellites and people. In November 1991, the 45th Space Wing was activated and assumed responsibility of managing operations at Patrick AFB and the Cape. The wing has the following four primary functions: providing resources for flight safety, range instrumentation, infrastructure, and scheduling for space and ballistic missile launches; responsibility for launch operations and support; supporting expeditionary and contingency readiness; and maintaining base and personnel support activities.

The 920th Rescue Wing, Air Force Reserve Command's premier combat search and rescue unit, is also part of Patrick AFB. Airmen of the 920th are capable of locating and recovering armed forces personnel anywhere in the world during wartime and peacetime military operations. Other missions include search and rescue support for civilians, participating in humanitarian and disaster relief operations, and security surveillance of the Eastern Range during launches. The motto of the 920th is, "These things we do, that others may live."

The Jupiter was an Intermediate Range Ballistic Missile (IRBM) developed initially by the US Army but later transferred to the Air Force. Jupiter served as a weapon system and a space booster, launching "monkeynaut" Gordo into space in December 1958 and Able and Baker together in May 1959.

The Thor was America's first IRBM. It was deployed in England from 1958 to 1963. Thor was a single-stage Air Force missile capable of being transported by aircraft along with its trailer, which also served as its erecting arm. Variations of the Thor with upper stages and small solid-fueled rocket motors attached at its base served as boosters for launching many satellites and space probes.

The Atlas was the first ICBM declared operational by the United States. Later versions of Atlas carried satellites and astronauts into space. A heavily modified variation of Atlas is still in service today. It is due to the development of the Atlas ICBM that the solvent WD-40 exists today. Testing of the Atlas was conducted from multiple launch complexes at the Cape Canaveral launch area.

Titan I was the first true multistage ICBM developed by the United States. Only operational from 1962 to 1965, the Titan I supplemented the Atlas ICBM missile system. The Titan II ICBM would later replace Titan I. The role of Patrick AFB in the development of Titan I and Titan II involved conducting test launches from Launch Complexes 15, 16, 19, and 20 at the Cape Canaveral launch area.

The Scout was a versatile high-altitude research vehicle that could be fitted together in three- or four-stage combinations as needed to support various missions. It used many "off the shelf" items for payload handling and data recovery to keep costs down and was often referred to as the "poor man's rocket." The Blue Scout was the Air Force version of the basic Scout.

Minuteman is a three-stage, solid-fueled ICBM. Minuteman missiles were tested from surface launch pads and from 80-foot-deep silos at the Cape Canaveral launch area between 1961 and 1970. Variations include the Minuteman I, II, and III. The Minuteman III is still operational today and is the only land-based ICBM in the United States.

The 45th Space Wing emblem is divided into blue and gold quadrants—blue for sky and space and gold for the excellence needed to conduct successful missions. The "Ts" represent continuous testing of space vehicles. The large globe represents the Earth, while the smaller one represents the Moon and planets. The flight arrows show the normal path of vehicles launched from the Eastern Range, including flights to the Moon and beyond.

Headquartered at Patrick AFB, the command staff of the 45th Space Wing oversees operations at the base and nearby CCAFS. The wing's mission statement is "One team . . . Delivering Assured Space Launch, Range and Combat Capabilities for the Nation." Its motto is "Control of the Battlefield Begins here," and the wing's vision is to be the "World's Premier Gateway to Space." (Author's collection.)

To perform its mission, the 45th Space Wing is organized into four major groups: the Launch Group conducts mission assurance support for the launch vehicle and the spacecraft from the time they arrive through launch; the Operations Group operates and maintains all Eastern Range assets including communications equipment, weather instrumentation, and operations at the airfield; the Mission Support Group provides assistance and support to assure success of all operations; and the Medical Group serves to "provide compassionate, high-quality care, ensuring mission ready forces and healthy families." The 45th Space Wing has supported a variety of launch vehicles in numerous ways since it was activated in 1991. Models of some are displayed in the lobby of its headquarters building. Pictured are, from left to right, Titan IVB, Atlas IIAS, Atlas V 400, Delta II, and Delta IV Heavy. Not shown are the Space Shuttle, Atlas Centaur, variations of the Atlas V and Delta IV, Aries X-1, Polaris, Poseidon, Trident, Pershing, Chevaline, Penguin, Ariane, Loft, Starbird, and Falcon 9 variants. The future promises to bring more new launch vehicles.

Patrick AFB 45th Space Wing personnel serve "on console" at the Morrell Operations Center's (MOC) Control Room, CCAFS. They monitor operations during countdowns and launches. Formerly called the Range Operations Control Center, the facility was renamed the MOC in November 2007 in honor of the late Maj. Gen. Jimmey R. Morrell, the first commander of the 45th Space Wing from November 1991 to June 1993.

The MOC is the nerve center for all launches, security, flight safety, weather, and range operations. Personnel working at the MOC monitor everything from weather to boats or aircraft that might venture into an area cleared for safety prior to a launch. Following a launch, the MOC personnel and equipment track the vehicle and monitor its performance.

The Atlas Centaur Space Launch Vehicle consisted of an Atlas booster with a Centaur upper stage. The upper stage was a small rocket attached to the payload being carried and used to propel it farther after the main booster rocket had burned all its fuel and was jettisoned. The engine of the upper stage fired to boost the payload to its proper altitude, or to accelerate an interplanetary probe to escape velocity in order to break away from Earth and venture out into the solar system. The Centaur burned liquid hydrogen and oxygen as fuel and was jettisoned when no longer needed. Launches using the Atlas Centaur combination occurred from Launch Complex 36 at CCAFS from 1962 to 1994. Besides numerous communication satellites, the Atlas Centaur also launched the Surveyor spacecraft that soft-landed on the Moon, and sent probes to explore the planets Mercury, Venus, and Mars. A popular phrase heard when launch of an Atlas Centaur approached was "Go Atlas, Go Centaur!" Centaur was also used with Titan boosters and is still in use today.

Three 115-ton, 800-horsepower diesel locomotives were used at CCAFS. Two of these locomotives worked in tandem to move components of Titan III and Titan IV rockets between assembly buildings and launch pads at CCAFS. Prior to moving rockets, they were in service during the Korean Conflict, with one reportedly receiving a symbolic Purple Heart from its crew after being hit by enemy fire.

The Titan III and larger Titan IV space launch vehicles lifted off from Launch Complexes 40 and 41 at CCAFS. These big boosters were used for heavy military payloads intended for Earth orbit and also for scientific probes such as *Viking* and *Voyager* spacecraft. The last launch of a Titan was in 2005.

A Delta II rocket lifts off from Launch Complex 17A at CCAFS in September 2006. It carried a new generation of Global Positioning System (GPS) satellite into orbit. The new GPS provided additional military and civilian signals to increase accuracy and enhance performance for navigational device users around the world. The last Delta II flew from CCAFS in 2011.

This is a close-up view of a 9.5-foot-diameter payload fairing on a Delta II rocket. Note the acronym JCWS on the tower, which stood for Johnson Controls World Services. JCWS was a company that supported launch operations at CCAFS. JCWS was pronounced "jaws," which explains the shark's mouth and eyes on the fairing. The acronym MDA stood for Missile Defense Agency.

Aircraft from the 920th Rescue Wing at Patrick AFB were part of the total-force effort to provide astronaut emergency rescue, as well as public safety support, during all manned Space Shuttle flights from Kennedy Space Center. Here, a Marine C-130 refuels a 920th HH-60G Pave Hawk helicopter near the shuttle's launch pad. (Courtesy of 920th Rescue Wing, Patrick AFB.)

Two 920th Rescue Wing HH-60G Pave Hawk Helicopters and the USNS *Waters*, a Launch Area Support Ship, patrol near the launch of a Trident ballistic missile from a submerged submarine. These tests are conducted miles off the coast of Patrick AFB. The Naval Ordnance Test Unit oversees submarine and related operations utilizing Port Canaveral and all Eastern Range assets. (Courtesy of 920th Rescue Wing, Patrick AFB.)

The Delta IV Heavy is one of several versions of the Delta IV boosters that fly from Launch Complex 37 at CCAFS. Depending on the weight of the payload going into space, two additional booster rockets can be attached, which form the "Heavy" version. Delta IVs can also fly with only the center core booster if that is all that is required.

The Atlas V rocket is the current variation of the Atlas booster used to launch satellites from CCAFS. This March 2013 liftoff from Launch Complex 41 contained an Air Force Space-Based Infrared System satellite for detecting ballistic missile launches anywhere in the world. A helicopter from the 920th Rescue Wing is seen flying in support of the launch. (Courtesy of 920th Rescue Wing, Patrick AFB.)

Airmen from the 920th Rescue Wing perform a water rescue demonstration using one of the Wing's HH-60G Pave Hawk helicopters during an air show in Cocoa Beach in 2011. The 920th Rescue Wing was also celebrating 50 years (1961 to 2011) of support for manned spaceflight in the role of "guardians of the astronauts." (Courtesy of 920th Rescue Wing, Patrick AFB.)

A workhorse for nearly 50 years, this HC-130P/N King aircraft, No. 65-00976, has been retired to the "boneyard" at Davis-Monthan AFB in Arizona. The aircraft served with the 920th Rescue Wing at Patrick AFB. It had more than 16,000 flight hours of service refueling helicopters and performing other duties in support of search and rescue efforts at home and in such far-off places as Iraq and Afghanistan. (Courtesy of 920th Rescue Wing, Patrick AFB.)

The 920th Rescue Wing provided rescue support for all manned Space Shuttle missions launched from Kennedy Space Center. The wing also provided security surveillance of the Eastern Range during unmanned launches from CCAFS. Here, five Air Force HC-130P/N King and one Marine HC-130P/N King aircraft wait on standby at Patrick AFB. (Courtesy of 920th Rescue Wing, Patrick AFB.)

In December 2000, ownership of the Cape Canaveral Lighthouse was transferred from the Coast Guard to the Air Force. Maintenance of the structure and surrounding grounds is the responsibility of the 45th Space Wing. The Coast Guard continues to service the beacon at the top, which remains a functioning navigational aid.

Propelled by the civil rights movement in the 1960s and to counteract a national policy of segregation and inequality, the Department of Defense (DoD) mandated race relations training in 1971. An inter-service task force, chaired by Air Force Maj. Gen. Lucius Theus, led to the establishment of the Defense Race Relations Institute (DRRI) at Patrick AFB. The institute was later renamed Defense Equal Opportunity Management Institute (DEOMI) in 1979. (Courtesy of DEOMI.)

Since its inception in 1971, DRRI and DEOMI have enhanced mission readiness by fostering positive human relations throughout the DoD. That mandate has been carried from Patrick AFB to all branches of the military services by more than 45,000 DEOMI students, beginning with the first graduating class shown here. These principles maximize organizational cohesion and maintain the highest degree of mission readiness while maintaining the DoD reputation as a place where all individuals have dignity and worth. (Courtesy of DEOMI.)

The Airmen's Memorial is dedicated in memory of all airmen who gave their lives in service to the country. The memorial was made possible in 1987 by contributions from military and civilian organizations near Patrick AFB. Another plaque near the Airmen's Memorial is dedicated to the five crewmembers of *Jolly 18*, a CH-3 helicopter that crashed while supporting a Trident missile launch from a submarine near the coast of Cape Canaveral.

This is a monument at the Memorial Plaza for five Patrick AFB airmen who died in an explosion at Khobar Towers in Saudi Arabia on June 25, 1996. Members of the 1st Rescue Group who died in the bombing were Capt. Christopher J. Adams, Capt. Leland Haun, M.Sgt. Michael Heiser, Staff Sgt. Kevin Johnson, and Airman First Class Justin Wood. The monument was dedicated on June 25, 2000.

The mascot for the 45th Space Wing is "Sharky" the shark. He attends many functions on base and in the local community. Wing personnel are known as sharks, with the commander as "Shark One." As with any team mascot, Sharky is a source of pride, a champion of the fighting spirit and dedication to duty of wing members. GO SHARKS!

Patrick, the Air Force base that was once a Navy facility and now named for a distinguished Army general, has had a long and unique history thus far. The men and women, military and civilian, currently assigned to Patrick AFB continue to add to the legacy of the base. The work they do at the base and nearby CCAFS keeps this the "World's Premier Gateway to Space."

DISCOVER THOUSANDS OF LOCAL HISTORY BOOKS
FEATURING MILLIONS OF VINTAGE IMAGES

Arcadia Publishing, the leading local history publisher in the United States, is committed to making history accessible and meaningful through publishing books that celebrate and preserve the heritage of America's people and places.

Find more books like this at
www.arcadiapublishing.com

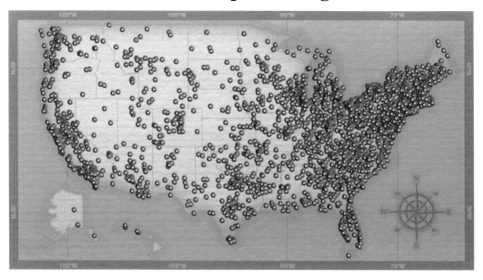

Search for your hometown history, your old stomping grounds, and even your favorite sports team.